THE
ASCENT OF MAN

BY

MATHILDE BLIND

THE ASCENT OF MAN.

PRELUDE.

WINGS.
Ascend, oh my Soul, with the wings of the lark ascend!
Soaring away and away far into the blue.
Or with the shrill seagull to the breakers bend,
Or with the bee, where the grasses and field-flowers blend,
Drink out of golden cups of the honey-dew.
Ascend, oh my Soul, on the wings of the wind as it blows,
Striking wild organ-blasts from the forest trees,
Or on the zephyr bear love of the rose to the rose,[4]
Or with the hurricane sower cast seed as he goes
Limitless ploughing the leagues of the sibilant seas.
Ascend, oh my Soul, on the wings of the choral strain,
Invisible tier above tier upbuilding sublime;
Note as it scales after note in a rhythmical chain
Reaching from chaos and welter of struggle and pain,
Far into vistas empyreal receding from time.
Ascend! take wing on the thoughts of the Dead, my Soul,
Breathing in colour and stone, flashing through epic and song:
Thoughts that like avalanche snows gather force as they roll,
Mighty to fashion and knead the phenomenal throng
Of generations of men as they thunder along.[5]

THE ASCENT OF MAN.

PART I.

[6]

As compressed within the bounded shell
Boundless Ocean seems to surge and swell,
Haunting echoes of an infinite whole
Moan and murmur through Man's finite soul.[7]

CHAUNTS OF LIFE.

I.
Struck out of dim fluctuant forces and shock of electrical vapour,
Repelled and attracted the atoms flashed mingling in union primeval,
And over the face of the waters far heaving in limitless twilight
Auroral pulsations thrilled faintly, and, striking the blank heaving surface,
The measureless speed of their motion now leaped into light on the waters.
And lo, from the womb of the waters, upheaved in volcanic convulsion,[8]
Ribbed and ravaged and rent there rose bald peaks and the rocky
Heights of confederate mountains compelling the fugitive vapours
To take a form as they passed them and float as clouds through the azure.
Mountains, the broad-bosomed mothers of torrents and rivers perennial,
Feeding the rivers and plains with patient persistence, till slowly,
In the swift passage of æons recorded in stone by Time's graver,
There germ grey films of the lichen and mosses and palm-ferns gigantic,
And jungle of tropical forest fantastical branches entwining,

And limitless deserts of sand and wildernesses primeval.[9]

II.
Lo, moving o'er chaotic waters,
Love dawned upon the seething waste,
Transformed in ever new avatars
It moved without or pause or haste:
Like sap that moulds the leaves of May
It wrought within the ductile clay.
And vaguely in the pregnant deep,
Clasped by the glowing arms of light
From an eternity of sleep
Within unfathomed gulfs of night
A pulse stirred in the plastic slime
Responsive to the rhythm of Time.
Enkindled in the mystic dark
Life built herself a myriad forms,
And, flashing its electric spark
Through films and cells and pulps and worms,[10]
Flew shuttlewise above, beneath,
Weaving the web of life and death.
And multiplying in the ocean,
Amorphous, rude, colossal things
Lolled on the ooze in lazy motion,
Armed with grim jaws or uncouth wings;
Helpless to lift their cumbering bulk
They lurch like some dismasted hulk.
And virgin forest, verdant plain,
The briny sea, the balmy air,
Each blade of grass and globe of rain,
And glimmering cave and gloomy lair
Began to swarm with beasts and birds,
With floating fish and fleet-foot herds.
The lust of life's delirious fires
Burned like a fever in their blood,
Now pricked them on with fierce desires,
Now drove them famishing for food,[11]
To seize coy females in the fray,
Or hotly hunted hunt for prey.
And amorously urged them on
In wood or wild to court their mate,
Proudly displaying in the sun
With antics strange and looks elate,
The vigour of their mighty thews
Or charm of million-coloured hues.
There crouching 'mid the scarlet bloom,
Voluptuously the leopard lies,
And through the tropic forest gloom
The flaming of his feline eyes
Stirs with intoxicating stress
The pulses of the leopardess.
Or two swart bulls of self-same age
Meet furiously with thunderous roar,
And lash together, blind with rage,

2

And clanging horns that fain would gore[12]
Their rival, and so win the prize
Of those impassive female eyes.
Or in the nuptial days of spring,
When April kindles bush and brier,
Like rainbows that have taken wing,
Or palpitating gems of fire,
Bright butterflies in one brief day
Live but to love and pass away.
And herds of horses scour the plains,
The thickets scream with bird and beast
The love of life burns in their veins,
And from the mightiest to the least
Each preys upon the other's life
In inextinguishable strife.
War rages on the teeming earth;
The hot and sanguinary fight
Begins with each new creature's birth:
A dreadful war where might is right;[13]
Where still the strongest slay and win,
Where weakness is the only sin.
There is no truce to this drawn battle,
Which ends but to begin again;
The drip of blood, the hoarse death-rattle,
The roar of rage, the shriek of pain,
Are rife in fairest grove and dell,
Turning earth's flowery haunts to hell.
A hell of hunger, hatred, lust,
Which goads all creatures here below,
Or blindworm wriggling in the dust,
Or penguin in the Polar snow:
A hell where there is none to save,
Where life is life's insatiate grave.
And in the long portentous strife,
Where types are tried even as by fire,
Where life is whetted upon life
And step by panting step mounts higher,[14]
Apes lifting hairy arms now stand
And free the wonder-working hand.
They raise a light, aërial house
On shafts of widely branching trees,
Where, harboured warily, each spouse
May feed her little ape in peace,
Green cradled in his heaven-roofed bed,
Leaves rustling lullabies o'erhead.
And lo, 'mid reeking swarms of earth
Grim struggling in the primal wood,
A new strange creature hath its birth:
Wild—stammering—nameless—shameless—nude;
Spurred on by want, held in by fear,
He hides his head in caverns drear.
Most unprotected of earth's kin,
His fight for life that seems so vain[15]
Sharpens his senses, till within
The twilight mazes of his brain,

3

Like embryos within the womb,
Thought pushes feelers through the gloom.
And slowly in the fateful race
It grows unconscious, till at length
The helpless savage dares to face
The cave-bear in his grisly strength;
For stronger than its bulky thews
He feels a force that grows with use.
From age to dumb unnumbered age,
By dim gradations long and slow,
He reaches on from stage to stage,
Through fear and famine, weal and woe
And, compassed round with danger, still
Prolongs his life by craft and skill.
With cunning hand he shapes the flint,
He carves the horn with strange device,[16]
He splits the rebel block by dint
Of effort—till one day there flies
A spark of fire from out the stone:
Fire which shall make the world his own.[17]

III.
And from the clash of warring Nature's strife
Man day by day wins his imperilled life;
For, goaded on by want, he hunts the roe,
Chases the deer, and lays the wild boar low.
In his rude boat made of the hollow trees
He drifts adventurous on the unoared seas,
And, as he tilts upon the rocking tide,
Catches the glistening fish that flash and glide
Innumerably through the waters wide.
He'll fire the bush whose flames shall help him fel
The trunks to prop his roof, where he may dwell
Beside the bubbling of a crystal well,
Sheltered from drenching rains or noxious glare
When the sun holds the zenith. Delving there,
His cumbered wife, whose multifarious toil
Seems never done, breaks the rich virgin soil,[18]
And in the ashes casts the casual seeds
Of feathered grass and efflorescent weeds;
When, as with thanks, the bounteous earth one morn
Returns lush blades of life-sustaining corn.
And while the woman digs and plants, and twines
To precious use long reeds and pliant bines,
He—having hit the brown bird on the wing,
And slain the roe—returns at evening,
And gives his spoil unto her, to prepare
The succulent, wildwood scented, simmering fare,
While with impatient sniffs and eager-eyed
His bronze-limbed children gather to his side.
And, when the feast is done, all take their ease,
Lulled by the sing-song of the evening breeze
And murmuring undertones of many-foliaged trees;
While here and there through rifts of green the sky

4

Casts its blue glance like an all-seeing eye.
But though by stress of want and poignant need
Man tames the wolf-sprung hound and rearing steed,
Pens up the ram, and yokes the deep-horned ox,[19]
And through wide pastures shepherds woolly flocks;
Though age by age, through discipline of toil,
Man wring a richer harvest from the soil,
And in the grim and still renewing fight
Slays loathly worms and beasts of gruesome might
By the close-knitted bondage of the clan,
Which adding up the puny strength of man
Makes thousands move with one electric thrill
Of simultaneous, energetic will;
Yet still behind the narrow borderland
Where in security he seems to stand,
His apprehensive life is compassed round
By baffling mysteries he cannot sound,
Where, big with terrors and calamities,
The future like a foe in ambush lies:
A muffled foe, that seems to watch and wait
With the Medusa eyes of stony fate.—
Great floods o'erwhelm and ruin his ripening grain,
His boat is shattered by the hurricane,[20]
From the rent cloud the tameless lightning springs—
Heaven's flame-mouthed dragon with a roar of wings—
And fires his hut and simple household things;
Until before his horror-stricken eyes
The stored-up produce of long labour lies,
A heap of ashes smoking 'neath the skies.—
Or now the pastures where his flocks did graze,
Parched, withered, shrivelled by the imminent blaze
Of the great ball of fire that glares above,
Glow dry like iron heated in a stove;
Turning upon themselves, the tortured sheep,
With blackening tongues, drop heap on gasping heap,
Their rotting flesh sickens the wind that moans
And whistles poisoned through their chattering bones;
While the thin shepherd, staring sick and gaunt,
Will search the thorns for berries, or yet haunt[21]
The stony channels of some river-bed
Where filtering fresh perchance a liquid thread
Of water may run clear.—Now dark o'erhead,
Thickening with storm, the wintry clouds will loom,
And wrap the land in weeds of mournful gloom;
Shrouding the sun and every lesser light
Till earth with all her aging woods grows white,
And hurrying streams stop fettered in their flight.
Then famished beasts freeze by the frozen lakes,
And thick as leaves dead birds bestrew the brakes;
And, cowering blankly by the flickering flame,
Man feels a presence without form or name,
When by the bodies of his speechless dead
In barbarous woe he bows his stricken head.
Then in the hunger of his piteous love
He sends his thought, winged like a carrier dove—

5

Through the unanswering silence void and vast,
Whence from dim hollows blows an icy blast—
To bring some sign, some little sign at last,[22]
From his lost chiefs—the beautiful, the brave—
Vanished like bubbles on a breaking wave,
Lost in the unfathomed darkness of the grave.
When, lo, behold beside him in the night,—
Softly beside him, like the noiseless light
Of moonbeams moving o'er the glimmering floor
That come unbidden through the bolted door,—
The lonely sleeper sees the lost one stand
Like one returned from some dim, distant land,
Bending towards him with his outstretched hand.
But when he fain would grasp it in his own,
He melts into thin moonshine and is gone—
A spirit now, who on the other shore
Of death hunts happily for evermore.—
A Son of Life, but dogged, while he draws breath,
By her inseparable shadow—death,
Man, feeble Man, whom unknown Fates appal,
With prayer and praise seeks to propitiate all
The spirits, who, for good or evil plight,
Bless him in victory or in sickness smite.[23]
Those are his Dead who, wrapped in grisly shrouds,
Now ride phantasmal on the rushing clouds,
Souls of departed chiefs whose livid forms
He sees careering on the reinless storms,
Wild, spectral huntsmen who tumultuously,
With loud halloo and shrilly echoing cry,
Follow the furious chase, with the whole pack
Of shadowy hounds fierce yelping in the track
Of wolves and bears as shadowy as the hosts
Who lead once more as unsubstantial ghosts
Their lives of old as restlessly they fly
Across the wildernesses of the sky.
When the wild hunt is done, shall they not rest
Their heads upon some swan-white maiden's breast,
And quaff their honeyed mead with godlike zest
In golden-gated Halls whence they may see
The earth and marvellous secrets of the Sea
Whereon the clouds will lie with grey wings furled,[24]
And in whose depths, voluminously curled,
The serpent looms whose girth engirds the world?
Far, far above now in supernal power
Those spirits rule the sunshine and the shower!
How shall he win their favour; yea, how move
To pity the unpitying gods above,
The Dæmon rulers of life's fitful dream,
Who sway men's destinies, and still would seem
To treat them lightly as a game of chance,
The sport of whim and blindfold circumstance—
The irresponsible, capricious gods,
So quick to please or anger; whose sharp rods
Are storms and lightnings launched from cloven skies;
Who feast upon the shuddering victim's cries,

6

The smell of blood, and human sacrifice.
But ever as Man grows they grow with him;
Terrific, cruel, gentle, bright, or dim,
With eyes of dove-like mercy, hands of wrath,
Procession-like, they hover o'er his path[25]
And, changing with the gazer, borrow light
From their rapt devotee's adoring sight.
And Ormuzd, Ashtaroth, Osiris, Baal—
Love spending gods and gods of blood and wail—
Look down upon their suppliant from the skies
With his own magnified, responsive eyes.
For Man, from want and pressing hunger freed,
Begins to feel another kind of need,
And in his shaping brain and through his eyes
Nature, awakening, sees her blue-arched skies;
The Sun, his life-begetter, isled in space;
The Moon, the Measurer of his span of days;
The immemorial stars who pierce his night
With inklings of things vast and infinite.
All shows of heaven and earth that move and pass
Take form within his brain as in a glass.
The tidal thunder of the sea now roars
And breaks symphonious on a hundred shores;
The fitful flutings of the vagrant breeze
Strike gusts of sound from virgin forest trees;[26]
White leaping waters of wild cataracts fall
From crag and jag in lapses musical,
And streams meandering amid daisied leas
Throb with the pulses of tumultuous seas.
From hills and valleys smoking mists arise,
Steeped in pale gold and amethystine dyes.
The land takes colour from him, and the flowers
Laugh in his path like sun-dyed April showers.
The moving clouds in calm or thunderstorm,
All shows of things in colour, sound, or form
Moulded mysteriously, are freshly wrought
Within the fiery furnace of his thought.[27]

IV.
No longer Nature's thrall,
Man builds the city wall
That shall withstand her league of levelling storms;
He builds tremendous tombs
Where, hid in hoarded glooms,
His dead defy corruption with her worms:
High towers he rears and bulks of glowing stone,
Where the king rules upon a golden throne.
Creature of hopes and fears,
Of mirth and many tears,
He makes himself a thousand costly altars,
Whence smoke of sacrifice,
Fragrant with myrrh and spice,
Ascends to heaven as the flame leaps and falters;
Where, like a king above the Cloud control,

7

God sits enthroned and rules Man's subject soul.[28]
Yet grievous here below
And manifold Man's woe;
Though he can stay the flood and bind the waters,
His hand he shall not stay
That bids him sack and slay
And turn the waving fields to fields of slaughters;
And, as he reaps War's harvest grim and gory,
Commits a thousand crimes and calls it glory.
Vast empires fall and rise,
As when in sunset skies
The monumental clouds lift flashing towers
With turrets, spires, and bars
Lit by confederate stars
Till the bright rack dissolves in flying showers:
Kingdoms on kingdoms have their fleeting day,
Dazzle the conquered world, and pass away.
In golden Morning lands
The blazing crowns change hands,
From mystic Ind to fleshly Babylon,[29]
Assyria, Palestine
Armed with her book divine,
Dread Persia whose fleet chariots charged and won
Pale Continents where prostrate monarchs kneel
Before the flash of her resistless steel.
As one by one they start
With proudly beating heart
Fast in the furious, fierce-contested race,
Where neck to neck they strain
Deliriously to gain
The winning post of power, the meed of praise;
Some drop behind, fall, or are trampled down
While the proud victor grasps the laurel crown.
Not only great campaigns
Shall glorify their reigns,
But high-towered cities wondrous to behold,
With gardens poised in air
Like bowers of Eden fair,
With brazen gates and shrines of beaten gold,[30]
And Palace courts whose constellated lights
Shine on black slaves and cringing satellites.
Eclipsing with her fate
Each power and rival state
With her unnumbered stretch of generations,
A sand-surrounded isle
Fed by the bounteous Nile,
Egypt confronts Sahara—sphinx of nations;
Taught by the floods that make or mar her shore,
She scans the stars and hoards mysterious lore.
Hers are imperial halls
With strangely scriptured walls
And long perspectives of memorial places,
Where the hushed daylight glows
On mute colossal rows
Of clawed wild beasts featured with female faces,[31]

8

And realmless kings inane whose stony eyes
Have watched the hour-glass of the centuries.
There in the rainless sands
The toil of captive hands,
That aye must do as their taskmaster bids,
Through years of dusty days
Brick by slow brick shall raise
The incarnate pride of kings—the Pyramids—
Linked with some name synonymous with slaughter
Time has effaced like a name writ in water.
For ever with fateful shocks,
Roar as of hurtling rocks,
Start fresh embattled hosts with flags unfurled,
To meet on battle-fields
With clash of spears and shields,
Widowing the world of men to win the world:
The hissing air grows dark with iron rain,
And groans the earth beneath her sheaves of slain.[32]
Triumphant o'er them all,
See crowns and sceptres fall
Before the arms of iron-soldered legions;
As Capitolian Rome
Across the salt sea foam
Orders her Cæsars to remotest regions:
From silver Spain and Albion's clouded seas
To the fair shrines and marble mines of Greece.
Pallas unmatched in war,
To her triumphal car
Rome chains fallen despots and discrownèd queens
With many a rampant beast,
Birds from the gorgeous East,
And wool-haired Nubians torn from tropic scenes;
There huge barbarians from Druidic woods
Tower ominous o'er the humming multitudes;
For still untamed and free
In loathed captivity,
Their spirits bend not to the conqueror's yoke,[33]
Though for a Roman sight
They must in mimic fight
Give wounds in play and deal Death's mortal stroke,
While round the arena rings the fierce applause
Voluptuous, as their bubbling life-blood flows
In streams of purple rain
From hecatombs of slain
Saluting Cæsar still with failing breath,
But in their dying souls
Undying hate, which rolls
From land to land the avalanche of Death,
That, gathering volume as it sweeps along,
Pours down the Alps throng on unnumbered throng.
From northern hills and plains
Storm-lashed by driving rains,
From moorland wastes and depths of desolate wood,[34]
From many an icebound shore,
The human torrents pour,

9

Horde following upon horde as flood on flood,
Avengers of the slain they come, they come,
And break in thunder on the walls of Rome.
A trembling people waits
As, surging through its gates,
Break the fierce Goths with trumpet-blasts of doom;
And many a glorious shrine
Begins to flare and shine,
And many a palace flames up through the gloom,
Kindled like torches by relentless wrath
To light the Spoiler on destruction's path.
Yea, with Rome's ravished walls,
The old world tottering falls
And crumbles into ruin wide and vast;[35]
The Empire seems to rock
As with an earthquake's shock,
And vassal provinces look on aghast;
As realms are split and nation rent from nation,
The globe seems drifting to annihilation.[36]

V.
"Peace on earth and good will unto Men!"
Came the tidings borne o'er wide dominions;
The glad tidings thrilled the world as when
Spring comes fluttering on the west wind's pinions,
When her voice is heard
Warbling through each bird,
And a new-born hope
Throbs through all things infinite in scope.
"Peace on earth and good will!" came the word
Of the Son of Man, the Man of Sorrow—
But the peace turned to a flaming sword,
Turned to woe and wailing on the morrow
When with gibes and scorns,
Crowned with barren thorns,
Gashed and crucified,
On the Cross the tortured Jesus died.[37]
And the world, once full of flower-hung shrines,
Now forsakes old altars for the new,
Zeus grows faint and Venus' star declines
As Jehovah glorifies the Jew,
He whom—lit with awe—
God-led Moses saw,
Graving with firm hand
In his people's heart his Lord's command.
Holding Hells and Heavens in either hand
Comes the priest and comes the wild-eyed prophet,
Tells the people of some happier land,
Terrifies them with a burning Tophet;
Gives them creeds for bread
And warm roof o'erhead,
Gives for life's delight
Passports to the kingdom, spirit-bright.
And the people groaning everywhere

Hearken gladly to the wondrous story,[38]
How beyond this life of toil and care
They shall lead a life of endless glory:
Where beyond the dim
Earth-mists Seraphim,
Love-illumined, wait—
Hierarchies of angels at heaven's gate.
Let them suffer while they live below,
Bear in silence weariness and pain;
For the heavier is their earthly woe,
Verily the heavenlier is their gain
In the mansions where
Sorrow and despair,
Yea, all moan shall cease
With the moan of immemorial seas.
And to save their threatened souls from sin,
Save them from the world, the flesh, the devil,
Men and Women break from bonds of kin
And in cloistered cell draw bar on evil,[39]
Worship on their knees
Sacred Images,
And all Saints above,
The Madonna, mystic Rose of love.
Mystic Rose of Maiden Motherhood,
Moon of Hearts immaculately mild,
Beaming o'er the turbulent times and rude
With the promise of her blessèd Child:
Whom pale Monks adore,
Pining evermore
For the heaven of love
Which their homesick lives are dying of.
But the flame of mystical desires
Turns to fury fiercer than a leopard's,
Holy fagots blaze with kindling fires
As the priests, the people's careful shepherds,
In Heaven's awful name,
Set the pile on flame[40]
Where, for Conscience' sake,
Heretics burn chaunting at the stake.
Subterranean secrets of the prison,
Throbs of anguish in the crushing cell,
Torture-chambers of the Inquisition
Are the Church's antidotes to Hell.
Better rack them here,
Mutilate and sear,
Than their souls should go
To the place of everlasting woe.
And a lurid universal night,
Lit by quenchless fires for unquenched sages,
Thick with spectral broods that shun the light,
Looms impervious o'er the stifled ages
Where the blameless wise
Fall a sacrifice,
Fall as fell of old
The unspotted firstlings of the fold.[41]

And the violent feud of clashing creeds
Shatters empires and breaks realms asunder;
Cities tremble, sceptres shake like reeds
At the swift bolts of the Papal thunder;
Yea, the bravest quail,
Cast from out the pale
Of all Christendom
By the dread anathemas of Rome.
And like one misled by marish gleams
When he hears the shrill cock's note of warning,
Europe, starting from its trance of dreams,
Sees the first streak of the clear-eyed morning
As it broadening stands
Over ravaged lands
Where mad nations are
Locked in grip of fratricidal war.
Castles burn upon the vine-clad knolls,
Huts glow smouldering in the trampled meadows;[42]
And a hecatomb of martyred souls
Fills a queenly town with wail of widows
In those branded hours
When red-guttering showers
Splash by courts and stews
To the Bells of Saint Bartholomew's.
Seed that's sown upon the wanton wind
Shall be harvested in whirlwind rages,
For revenge and hate bring forth their kind,
And black crime must ever be the wages
Of a nation's crime
Time transmits to time,
Till the score of years
Is wiped out in floods of staunchless tears.
Yea, the anguish in a people's life
May have eaten out its heart of pity,
Bred in scenes of scarlet sin and strife,
Heartless splendours of a haughty city;[43]
Dark with lowering fate,
At the massive gate
Of its kings it may
Stand and knock with tragic hand one day.
For the living tomb gives up its dead,
Bastilles yawn, and chains are rent asunder,
Little children now and hoary head,
Man and maiden, meet in joy and wonder;
Throng on radiant throng,
Brave and blithe and strong,
Gay with pine and palm,
Fill fair France with freedom's thunder-psalm.
Free and equal—rid of king and priest—
The rapt nation bids each neighbour nation
To partake the sacramental feast
And communion of the Federation:
And electrified
Masses, far and wide,[44]
Thrill to hope and start

12

Vibrating as with one common heart.
From the perfumed South of amorous France
With her wreath of orange bloom and myrtle,
From old wizard woods of lost Romance
Soft with wail of wind and voice of turtle,
From the roaring sea
Of grey Normandy,
And the rich champaigns
Where the vine gads o'er Burgundian plains;
From the banks of the blue arrowy Rhone,
And from many a Western promontory,
From volcanic crags of cloven stone
Crowned with castles ivy-green in story;
From gay Gascon coasts
March fraternal hosts,
Equal hosts and free,
Pilgrims to the shrine of liberty.[45]
But king calls on king in wild alarms,
Troops march threatening through the vales and passes,
Barefoot Faubourgs at the cry to arms
On the frontier hurl their desperate masses:
The deep tocsin's boom
Fills the streets with gloom,
And with iron hand
The red Terror guillotines the land.
For the Furies of the sanguine past
Chase fair Freedom, struggling torn and baffled,
Till infuriate—turned to bay at last—
Rolled promiscuous on the common scaffold,
Vengeful she shall smite
A Queen's head bleached white,
And a courtesan's
Whose light hands once held the reins of France.[46]
She shall smite and spare not—yea, her own,
Her fair sons so pure from all pollution,
With their guiltless life-blood must atone
To the goddess of the Revolution;
Dying with a song
On their lips, her young
Ardent children end,
Meeting death even as one meets a friend.
And her daughter, in heroic shame,
Turned to Freedom's Moloch statue, crying:
"Liberty, what crimes done in thy name!"
Spake, and with her Freedom's self seemed dying
As she bleeding lay
'Neath Napoleon's sway:
Europe heard her knell
When on Waterloo the Empire fell.[47]

VI.
Woe, woe to Man and all his hapless brood!
No rest for him, no peace is to be found;
He may have tamed wild beasts and made the ground

Yield corn and wine and every kind of food;
He may have turned the ocean to his steed,
Tutored the lightning's elemental speed
To flash his thought from Ætna to Atlantic;
He may have weighed the stars and spanned the stream,
And trained the fiery force of panting steam
To whirl him o'er vast steppes, and heights gigantic:
But the storm-lashed world of feeling—
Love, the fount of tears unsealing,
Choruses of passion pealing—[48]
Lust, ambition, hatred, awe,
Clashing loudly with the law,
But the phantasms of the mind
Who shall master, yea, who bind!
What help is there without, what hope within
Of rescue from the immemorial strife?
What will redeem him from the spasm of life,
With all its devious ways of shame and sin?
What will redeem him from ancestral greeds,
Grey legacies of hate and hoar misdeeds,
Which from the guilty past Man doth inherit—
The past that is bound up with him, and part
Of the pulsations of his inmost heart,
And of the vital motions of his spirit?
Ages mazed in tortuous errors,
Ghostly fears, and haunting terrors,
Minds bewitched that served as mirrors
For the foulest fancies bred
In a fasting hermit's head,[49]
Such as cast a sickly blight
On all shapes of life and light.
Yea, panting and pursued and stung and driven,
The soul of Man flies on in deep distress,
As once across the world's harsh wilderness
Latona fled, chased by the Queen of heaven;
Flying across the homeless Universe
From the inveterate stroke of Juno's curse;
On whom even mother earth closed all her portals,
Refusing shelter in her cooing bowers,
Or rest upon her velvet couch of flowers,
To the most weary of all weary mortals.
Within whose earth-encumbered form,
Like two fair stars entwined in storm,
Or wings astir within the worm,
Feeling out for light and air,
Struggled that celestial pair,
Phœbus of unerring bow,
And chaste Dian fair as snow.[50]
Ah, who will harbour her? Ah, who will save
The fugitive from pangs that rack and tear;
Who, finding rest nor refuge anywhere,
Seems doomed to be her unborn offspring's grave;
The seed of Jove, murdered before their birth—
Did not the sea, more merciful than earth,
Bid Delos stand—that wandering isle of Ocean—

Stand motionless upon the moving foam,
To be the exile's wave-encircled home,
And lull her pains with leaves in drowsy motion,
Where the soft-boughed olive sighing
Bends above the woman lying
And in spasms of anguish crying,
Shuddering through her mortal frame,
As from dust is struck the flame
Which shall henceforth beam sublime
Through the firmament of Time?
Oh, balmy Island bedded on the brine,
Harbour of refuge on the tumbling seas,[51]
The fabulous bowers of the Hesperides
Ne'er bore such blooming gold as glows in thine:
Thou green Oasis on the tides of Time
Where no rude blast disturbs the azure clime;
Thou Paradise whence man can ne'er be driven,
Where, severed from the world-clang and the roar,
Still in the flesh he yet may reach that shore
Where want is not, and, like the dew from heaven,
There drops upon the fevered soul
The balm of Thought's divine control
And rapt absorption in the whole:
Delivery in the realm of art
Of the world-racked human heart—
Forms and hues and sounds that make
Life grow lovelier for their sake.
By sheer persistence, strenuous and slow,
The marble yields and, line by flowing line
And curve by curve, begins to swell and shine
Beneath the ring of each far-sighted blow:[52]
Until the formless block obeys the hand,
And at the mastering mind's supreme command
Takes form and radiates from each limb and feature
Such beauty as ne'er bloomed in mortal mould,
Whose face, out-smiling centuries, shall hold
Perfection's mirror up to 'prentice nature.
Not from out voluptuous ocean
Venus rose in balanced motion,
Goddess of all bland emotion;
But she leaped a shape of light,
Radiating love's delight,
From the sculptor's brain to be
Sphered in immortality.
New spirit-yearnings for a heavenlier mood
Call for a love more pitiful and tender,
And 'neath the painter's touch blooms forth in splendour
The image of transfigured motherhood.[53]
All hopes of all glad women who have smiled
In adoration on their first-born child
Here smile through one glad woman made immortal;
All tears of all sad women through whose heart
Has pierced the edge of sorrow's sevenfold dart
Lie weeping with her at death's dolorous portal.
For in married hues whose splendour

Bodies forth the gloom and grandeur
Of life's pageant, tragic, tender,
Common things transfigured flush
By the magic of the brush,
As when sun-touched raindrops glow,
Blent in one harmonious bow.
But see, he comes, Lord of life's changeful shows,
To whom the ways of Nature are laid bare,
Who looks on heaven and makes the heavens more fair,
And adds new sweetness to the perfumed rose;[54]
Who can unseal the heart with all its tears,
Marshal loves, hates, hopes, sorrows, joys, and fears
In quick procession o'er the passive pages;
Who has given tongue to silent generations
And wings to thought, so that long-mouldered nations
May call to nations o'er the abyss of ages:
The poet, in whose shaping brain
Life is created o'er again
With loftier raptures, loftier pain;
Whose mighty potencies of verse
Move through the plastic Universe,
And fashion to their strenuous will
The world that is creating still.
Do you hear it, do you hear it
Soaring up to heaven, or somewhere near it?
From the depths of life upheaving,
Clouds of earth and sorrow cleaving,
From despair and death retrieving,[55]
All triumphant blasts of sound
Lift you at one rhythmic bound
From the thraldom of the ground.
All the sweetness which the glowing
Violets waft to west winds blowing,
All the burning love-notes aching,
Rills and thrills of rapture shaking
Through the hearts that throb to breaking
Of the little nightingales;
Mellow murmuring waters streaming
Lakeward in long silver trails,
Crooning low while earth lies dreaming
To the moonlight-tangled vales;
Swish of rain on half-blown roses
Hoarding close their rich perfume,
Which the summer dawn uncloses
Sparkling in their morning bloom;
Convent peals o'er pastoral meadows,
Swinging through hay-scented air[56]
When the velvet-footed shadows
Call the hind to evening prayer.
Yea, all notes of woods and highlands;
Sea-fowls' screech round sphinx-like islands
Couched among the Hebrides;
Cuckoo calls through April showers,
When the green fields froth with flowers
And with bloom the orchard trees.

Boom of surges with their hollow
Refluent shock from cave to cave,
As the maddening spring tides follow
Moonstruck reeling wave o'er wave.
Yea, all rhythms of air and ocean
Married to the heart's emotion,
To the intervolved emotion
Of the heart for ever turning
In a whirl of bliss and pain,
Blending in symphonious strain
All the vague, unearthly yearning
Of the visionary brain.
[57]

All life's discords sweetly blending,
Heights on heights of being ascending,
Harmonies of confluent sound
Lift you at one rhythmic bound
From the thraldom of the ground;
Loosen all your bonds of birth,
Clogs of sense and weights of earth,
Bear you in angelic legions
High above terrestrial regions
Into ampler ether, where
Spirits breathe a finer air,
Where upon world altitudes
God-intoxicated moods
Fill you with beatitudes;
Till no longer cramped and bound
By the narrow human round,
All the body's barriers slide,
Which with cold obstruction hide
The supreme, undying, sole
Spirit struggling through the whole,[58]
And no more a thing apart
From the universal heart
Liberated by the grace
Of man's genius for a space,
Human lives dissolve, enlace
In a flaming world embrace.[59]

A SYMBOL.
Hurrying for ever in their restless flight
The generations of earth's teeming womb
Rise into being and lapse into the tomb
Like transient bubbles sparkling in the light;
They sink in quick succession out of sight
Into the thick insuperable gloom
Our futile lives in flashing by illume—
Lightning which mocks the darkness of the night.
Nay—but consider, though we change and die,
If men must pass shall Man not still remain?
As the unnumbered drops of summer rain
Whose changing particles unchanged on high,

17

Fixed, in perpetual motion, yet maintain
The mystic bow emblazoned on the sky.[60]

TIME'S SHADOW.
Thy life, O Man, in this brief moment lies:
Time's narrow bridge whereon we darkling stand,
With an infinitude on either hand
Receding luminously from our eyes.
Lo, there thy Past's forsaken Paradise
Subsideth like some visionary strand,
While glimmering faint, the Future's promised land,
Illusive from the abyss, seems fain to rise.
This hour alone Hope's broken pledges mar,
And Joy now gleams before, now in our rear,
Like mirage mocking in some waste afar,
Dissolving into air as we draw near.
Beyond our steps the path is sunny-clear,
The shadow lying only where we are.[61]
THE ASCENT OF MAN.

PART II.

[62]

"Love is for ever poor, and so far from being delicate and beautiful, as mankind imagined, he is squalid and withered ... homeless and unsandalled; he sleeps without covering before the doors, and in the unsheltered streets."—Plato.

[63]

THE PILGRIM SOUL.
Through the winding mazes of windy streets
Blindly I hurried I knew not whither,
Through the dim-lit ways of the brain thus fleets
A fluttering dream driven hither and thither.—
The fitful flare of the moon fled fast,
Like a sickly smile now seeming to wither,
Now dark like a scowl in the hurrying blast
As ominous shadows swept over the roofs
Where white as a ghost the scared moonlight had passed.
Curses came mingled with wails and reproofs,
With doors banging to and the crashing of glass,
With the baying of dogs and the clatter of hoofs,[64]
With the rush of the river as, huddling its mass
Of weltering water towards the deep ocean,
'Neath many-arched bridges its eddies did pass.
A hubbub of voices in savage commotion
Was mixed with the storm in a chaos of sound,
And thrilled as with ague in shuddering emotion
I fled as the hunted hare flees from the hound.
Past churches whose bells were tumultuously ringing
The year in, and clashing in concord around;

18

Past the deaf walls of dungeons whose curses seemed clinging
To the tempest that shivered and shrieked in amazement;
Past brightly lit mansions whence music and singing[65]
Came borne like a scent through the close-curtained casement,
To vaults in whose shadow wild outcasts were hiding
Their misery deep in the gloom of the basement.
By vociferous taverns where women were biding
With features all withered, distorted, aghast;
Some sullenly silent, some brutally chiding,
Some reeling away into gloom as I passed
On, on, through lamp-lighted and fountain-filled places,
Where throned in rich temples, resplendent and vast,
The Lord of the City is deafened with praises
As worshipping multitudes kneel as of old;
Nor care for the crowds of cadaverous faces,[66]
The men that are marred and the maids that are sold—
Inarticulate masses promiscuously jumbled
And crushed 'neath their Juggernaut idol of gold.
Lost lives of great cities bespattered and tumbled,
Black rags the rain soaks, the wind whips like a knout,
Were crouched in the streets there, and o'er them nigh stumbled
A swarm of light maids as they tripped to some rout.
The silk of their raiment voluptuously hisses
And flaps o'er the flags as loud laughing they flout
The wine-maddened men they ne'er satiate with kisses
For the pearls and the diamonds that make them more fair,
For the flash of large jewels that fire them with blisses,[67]
For the glitter of gold in the gold of their hair.
They smiled and they cozened, their bold eyes shone brightly
And lightened with laughter, as, lit by the flare
Of the wind-fretted gas-lamps, they footed it lightly,
Or, closely enlacing and bowered in gloom,
With mouth pressed to hot mouth, their parched lips drain nightly
The wine-cup of pleasure red-sealing their doom.
Brief lives like bright rockets which, aridly glowing,
Fall burnt out to ashes and reel to the tomb.
On, on, loud and louder the rough night was blowing,
Shrill singing was mixed with strange cries of despair;
And high overhead the black sky, redly glowing,[68]
Loomed over the city one ominous glare,
As dark yawning funnels from foul throats for ever
Belched smoke grimly flaming, which outraged the air.
On, on, by long quays where the lamps in the river
Were writhing like serpents that hiss ere they drown,
And poplars with palsy seemed coldly to shiver,
On, on, to the bare desert end of the town.
When lo! the wind stopped like a heart that's ceased beating,
And nought but the waters, white foaming and brown,
Were heard as to seaward their currents went fleeting.
But hark! o'er the lull breaks a desolate moan,
Like a little lost lamb's that is timidly bleating[69]
When, strayed from the shepherd, it staggers alone
By tracks which the mountain streams shake with their thunder,
Where death seems to gape from each boulder and stone.
I turned to the murmur: the clouds swept asunder

19

And wheeled like white sea-gulls around the white moon;
And the moon, like a white maid, looked down in mute wonder
On a boy whose wan eyelids were closed as in swoon.
Half nude on the ground he lay, wasted and chilly,
And torn as with thorns and sharp brambles of June;
His hair, like a flame which at twilight burns stilly,
In a halo of light round his temples was blown,
And his tears fell like rain on a storm-stricken lily[70]
Where he lay on the cold ground, abandoned, alone.
With heart moved towards him in wondering pity,
I tenderly seized his thin hand with my own:
Crying, "Child, say how cam'st thou so far from the city?
How cam'st thou alone in such pitiful plight,
All blood-stained thy feet, with rags squalid and gritty,
A waif by the wayside, unhoused in the night?"
Then rose he and lifted the bright locks, storm driven,
Which flamed round his forehead and clouded his sight,
And mournful as meres on a moorland at even
His blue eyes flashed wildly through tears as they fell.
Strange eyes full of horror, yet fuller of heaven,[71]
Like eyes that from heaven have looked upon hell.
The eyes of an angel whose depths show where, burning
And lost in the pit, toss the angels that fell.
"Ah," wailed he in tones full of agonized yearning,
Like the plaintive lament of a sickening dove
On a surf-beaten shore, whence it sees past returning
The wings of the wild flock fast fading above,
As they melt on the sky-line like foam-flakes in motion:
So sadly he wailed, "I am Love! I am Love!
"Behold me cast out as weed spurned of the ocean,
Half nude on the bare ground, and covered with scars
I perish of cold here;" and, choked with emotion,[72]
Gave a sob: at the low sob a shower of stars
Broke shuddering from heaven, pale flaming, and fell
Where the mid-city roared as with rumours of wars.
"Be these God's tears?" I cried, as my tears 'gan to well.
"Ah, Love, I have sought thee in temples and towers,
In shrines where men pray, and in marts where they sell;
"In tapestried chambers made tropic with flowers,
Where amber-haired women, soft breathing of spice,
Lay languidly lapped in the gold-dropping showers
"Which gladdened and maddened their amorous eyes.
I have looked for thee vainly in churches where beaming
The Saints glowed embalmed in a prism of dyes,[73]
"Where wave over wave the rapt music went streaming
With breakers of sound in full anthems elate.
I have asked, but none knew thee, or knew but thy seeming;
"A mask in thy likeness on high seats of state;
And they bound it with gold, and they crowned it with glory,
This thing they called love, which was bond slave to hate.
"And they bowed down before it with brown heads and hoary,
They worshipped it nightly, loud hymning its praise,
While out in the cold blast, none heeding its story,
"Love staggers, an outcast, with lust in its place."
Love shivered and sighed like a reed that is shaken,

And lifting his hunger-nipped face to my face:[74]
"Nay, if of the world I must needs die forsaken,
Say thou wilt not leave me to dearth and despair.
To thy heart, to thy home, let the exile be taken,
"And feed me and shelter——" "Where, outcast, ah, where?
Like thee I am homeless and spurned of all mortals;
The House of my fathers yawns wide to the air.
"Stalks desolation across the void portals,
Hope lies aghast on the ruinous floor,
The halls that were thronged once with star-browed immortals,
"With gods statue-still o'er the world-whirr and roar,
With fauns of the forest and nymphs of the river,
Are cleft as if lightning had struck to their core.[75]
"The luminous ceilings, where soaring for ever
Dim hosts of plumed angels smoked up to the sky,
With God-litten faces that yearned to the giver
"As vapours of morning the sun draws on high,
Now ravaged with rain hear the hollow winds whistle
Through rifts in the rafters which echo their cry.
"Blest walls that were vowed to the Virgin now bristle
With weeds of sick scarlet and plague-spotted moss,
And stained on the ground, choked with thorn and rank thistle,
"Rots a worm-eaten Christ on a mouldering Cross.
From the House of my fathers, distraught, broken-hearted,
With a pang of immense, irredeemable loss,[76]
"On my wearying pilgrimage blindly I started
To seek thee, oh Love, in high places and low,
And instead of the glories for ever departed,
"To warm my starved life in thy mightier glow.
For I deemed thee a Presence ringed round with all splendour,
With a sceptre in hand and a crown on thy brow;
"And, behold, thou art helpless—most helpless to tender
Thy service to others, who needest their care.
Yea, now that I find thee a weak child and slender,
"Exposed to the blast of the merciless air,
Like a lamb that is shorn, like a leaf that is shaken,
What, Love, now is left but to die in despair?[77]
"For Death is the mother of all the forsaken,
The grave a strait bed where she rocks them to rest,
And sleep, from whose silence they never shall waken,
"The balm of oblivion she sheds on their breast."
Then I seized him and led to the brink of the river,
Where two storm-beaten seagulls were fluttering west,
And the lamplight in drowning seemed coldly to shiver,
And clasping Love close for the leap from on high,
Said—"Let us go hence, Love; go home, Love, for ever;
"For life casts us forth, and Man dooms us to die."
As if stung by a snake the Child shuddered and started,
And clung to me close with a passionate cry:[78]
"Stay with me, stay with me, poor, broken-hearted;
Pain, if not pleasure, we two will divide;
Though with the sins of the world I have smarted,
"Though with the shame of the world thou art dyed,
Weak as I am, on thy breast I'll recover,
Worn as thou art, thou shalt bloom as my bride:

"Bloom as the flower of the World for the lover
Whom thou hast found in a lost little Child."
And as he kissed my lips over and over—
Child now, or Man, was it who thus beguiled?—
Even as I looked on him, Love, waxing slowly,
Grew as a little cloud, floating enisled,
Which spreads out aloft in the blue sky till solely
It fills the deep ether tremendous in height,
With far-flashing snow-peaks and pinnacles wholly[79]
Invisible, vanishing light within light.
So changing waxed Love—till he towered before me,
Outgrowing my lost gods in stature and might.
As he grew, as he drew me, a great awe came o'er me,
And stammering, I shook as I questioned his name;
But gently bowed o'er me, he soothèd and bore me,
Yea, bore once again to the haunts whence I came,
By dark ways and dreary, by rough roads and gritty,
To the penfolds of sin, to the purlieus of shame.
And lo, as we went through the woe-clouded city,
Where women bring forth and men labour in vain,
Weak Love grew so great in his passion of pity
That all who beheld him were born once again.[80]

SAVING LOVE.
Would we but love what will not pass away!
The sun that on each morning shines as clear
As when it rose first on the world's first year;
The fresh green leaves that rustle on the spray.
The sun will shine, the leaves will be as gay
When graves are full of all our hearts held dear,
When not a soul of those who loved us here,
Not one, is left us—creatures of decay.
Yea, love the Abiding in the Universe
Which was before, and will be after us.
Nor yet for ever hanker and vainly cry
For human love—the beings that change or die;
Die—change—forget: to care so is a curse,
Yet cursed we'll be rather than not care thus.[81]

NIRVANA.
Divest thyself, O Soul, of vain desire!
Bid hope farewell, dismiss all coward fears;
Take leave of empty laughter, emptier tears,
And quench, for ever quench, the wasting fire
Wherein this heart, as in a funeral pyre,
Aye burns, yet is consumed not. Years on years
Moaning with memories in thy maddened ears—
Let at thy word, like refluent waves, retire.
Enter thy soul's vast realm as Sovereign Lord,
And, like that angel with the flaming sword,
Wave off life's clinging hands. Then chains will fall
From the poor slave of self's hard tyranny—
And Thou, a ripple rounded by the sea,

22

In rapture lost be lapped within the All.[82]

MOTHERHOOD.
From out the font of being, undefiled,
A life hath been upheaved with struggle and pain;
Safe in her arms a mother holds again
That dearest miracle—a new-born child.
To moans of anguish terrible and wild—
As shrieks the night-wind through an ill-shut pane—
Pure heaven succeeds; and after fiery strain
Victorious woman smiles serenely mild.
Yea, shall she not rejoice, shall not her frame
Thrill with a mystic rapture! At this birth,
The soul now kindled by her vital flame
May it not prove a gift of priceless worth?
Some saviour of his kind whose starry fame
Shall bring a brightness to the darkened earth.[83]
THE ASCENT OF MAN.

PART III.

[84]

"Our spirits have climbed high
By reason of the passion of our grief,—
And from the top of sense, looked over sense
To the significance and heart of things
Rather than things themselves."
E. B. BROWNING.
[85]

THE LEADING OF SORROW.
Through a twilight land, a moaning region,
Thick with sighs that shook the trembling air,
Land of shadows whose dim crew was legion,
Lost I hurried, hunted by despair.
Quailed my heart like an expiring splendour,
Fitful flicker of a faltering fire,
Smitten chords which tempest-stricken render
Rhythms of anguish from a breaking lyre.
Love had left me in a land of shadows,
Lonely on the ruins of delight,
And I grieved with tearless grief of widows,
Moaned as orphans homeless in the night.
Love had left me knocking at Death's portal—
Shone his star and vanished from my sky—[86]
And I cried: "Since Love, even Love, is mortal,
Take, unmake, and break me; let me die."
Then, the twilight's grisly veils dividing,
Phantom-like there stole one o'er the plain,
Wavering mists for ever round it gliding
Hid the face I strove to scan in vain.

23

Spake the veiled one: "Solitary weeper,
'Mid the myriad mourners thou'rt but one:
Come, and thou shalt see the awful reaper,
Evil, reaping all beneath the sun."
On my hand the clay-cold hand did fasten
As it murmured—"Up and follow me;
O'er the thickly peopled earth we'll hasten,
Yet more thickly packed with misery."
And I followed: ever in the shadow
Of that looming form I fared along;
Now o'er mountains, now through wood and meadow,
Or through cities with their surging throng.[87]
With none other for a friend or fellow
Those relentless footsteps were my guide
To the sea-caves echoing with the hollow
Immemorial moaning of the tide.
Laughed the sunlight on the living ocean,
Danced and rocked itself upon the spray,
And its shivered beams in twinkling motion
Gleamed like star-motes in the Milky Way.
Lo, beneath those waters surging, flowing,
I beheld the Deep's fantastic bowers;
Shapes which seemed alive and yet were growing
On their stalks like animated flowers.
Sentient flowers which seemed to glow and glimmer
Soft as ocean blush of Indian shells,
White as foam-drift in the moony shimmer
Of those sea-lit, wave-pavilioned dells.
Yet even here, as in the fire-eyed panther,
In disguise the eternal hunger lay,[88]
For each feathery, velvet-tufted anther
Lay in ambush waiting for its prey.
Tiniest jewelled fish that flashed like lightning,
Blindly drawn, came darting through the wave,
When, a stifling sack above them tightening,
Closed the ocean-blossom's living grave.
Now we fared through forest glooms primeval
Through whose leaves the light but rarely shone,
Where the buttressed tree-trunks looked coeval
With the time-worn, ocean-fretted stone;
Where, from stem to stem their tendrils looping,
Coiled the lithe lianas fold on fold,
Or, in cataracts of verdure drooping,
From on high their billowy leafage rolled.
Where beneath the dusky woodland cover,
While the noon-hush holds all living things,[89]
Butterflies of tropic splendour hover
In a maze of rainbow-coloured wings:
Some like stars light up their own green heaven
Some are spangled like a golden toy,
Or like flowers from their foliage driven
In the fiery ecstasy of joy.
But, the forest slumber rudely breaking,
Through the silence rings a piercing yell;
At the cry unnumbered beasts, awaking,

24

With their howls the loud confusion swell.
'Tis the cry of some frail creature panting
In the tiger's lacerating grip;
In its flesh carnivorous teeth implanting,
While the blood smokes round his wrinkled lip.
'Tis the scream some bird in terror utters,
With its wings weighed down by leaden fears,
As from bough to downward bough it flutters
Where the snake its glistening crest uprears:[90]
Eyes of sluggish greed through rank weeds stealing,
Breath whose venomous fumes mount through the air,
Till benumbed the helpless victim, reeling,
Drops convulsed into the reptile snare.
Now we fared o'er sweltering wastes whose steaming
Clouds of tawny sand the wanderer blind.
Herds of horses with their long manes streaming
Snorted thirstily against the wind;
O'er the waste they scoured in shadowy numbers,
Gasped for springs their raging thirst to cool,
And, like sick men mocked in fevered slumbers,
Stoop to drink—and find a phantom pool.
What of antelopes crunched by the leopard?
What if hounds run down the timid hare?
What though sheep, strayed from the faithful shepherd,
Perish helpless in the lion's lair?[91]
The all-seeing sun shines on unheeding,
In the night shines the unruffled moon,
Though on earth brute myriads, preying, bleeding,
Put creation harshly out of tune.
Cried I, turning to the shrouded figure—
"Oh, in mercy veil this cruel strife!
Sanguinary orgies which disfigure
The green ways of labyrinthine life.
From the needs and greeds of primal passion,
From the serpent's track and lion's den,
To the world our human hands did fashion,
Lead me to the kindly haunts of men."
And through fields of corn we passed together,
Orange golden in the brooding heat,
Where brown reapers in the harvest weather
Cut ripe swathes of downward rustling wheat.
In the orchards dangling red and yellow,
Clustered fruit weighed down the bending sprays;[92]
On a hundred hills the vines grew mellow
In the warmth of fostering autumn days.
Through the air the shrilly twittering swallows
Flashed their nimble shadows on the leas;
Red-flecked cows were glassed in golden shallows,
Purple clover hummed with restless bees.
Herdsmen drove the cattle from the mountain,
To the fold the shepherd drove his flocks,
Village girls drew water from the fountain,
Village yokels piled the full-eared shocks.
From the white town dozing in the valley,
Round its vast Cathedral's solemn shade,

25

Citizens strolled down the walnut alley
Where youth courted and glad childhood played.
"Peace on earth," I murmured; "let us linger—
Here the wage of life seems good at least:"
As I spake the veiled One raised a finger
Where the moon broke flowering in the east.[93]
Faintly muttering from deep mountain ranges,
Muffled sounds rose hoarsely on the night,
As the crash of foundering avalanches
Wakes hoarse echoes in each Alpine height.
Near and nearer sounds the roaring—thunder,
Mortal thunder, crashes through the vale;
Lightning flash of muskets breaks from under
Groves once haunted by the nightingale.
Men clutch madly at each weapon—women,
Children crouch in cellars, under roofs,
For the town is circled by their foemen—
Shakes the ground with clang of trampling hoofs.
Shot on shot the volleys hiss and rattle,
Shrilly whistling fly the murderous balls,
Fiercely roars the tumult of the battle
Round the hard-contested, dear-bought walls.
Horror, horror! The fair town is burning,
Flames burst forth, wild sparks and ashes fly;[94]
With her children's blood the green earth's turning
Blood-red—blood-red, too, the cloud-winged sky.
Crackling flare the streets: from the lone steeple
The great clock booms forth its ancient chime,
And its dolorous quarters warn the people
Of the conquering troops that march with time.
Fallen lies the fair old town, its houses
Charred and ruined gape in smoking heaps;
Here with shouts a ruffian band carouses,
There an outraged woman vainly weeps.
In the fields where the ripe corn lies mangled,
Where the wounded groan beneath the dead,
Friend and foe, now helplessly entangled,
Stain red poppies with a guiltier red.
There the dog howls o'er his perished master,
There the crow comes circling from afar;
All vile things that batten on disaster
Follow feasting in the wake of war.[95]
Famine follows—what they ploughed and planted
The unhappy peasants shall not reap;
Sickening of strange meats and fever haunted,
To their graves they prematurely creep.
"Hence"—I cried in unavailing pity—
"Let us flee these scenes of monstrous strife,
Seek the pale of some imperial city
Where the law rules starlike o'er man's life."
Straightway floating o'er blue sea and river,
We were plunged into a roaring cloud,
Wherethrough lamps in ague fits did shiver
O'er the surging multitudinous crowd.
Piles of stone, their cliff-like walls uprearing,

Flashed in luminous lines along the night;
Jets of flame, spasmodically flaring,
Splashed black pavements with a sickly light;
Fabulous gems shone here, and glowing coral,
Shimmering stuffs from many an Eastern loom,[96]
And vast piles of tropic fruits and floral
Marvels seemed to mock November's gloom.
But what prowls near princely mart and dwelling,
Whence through many a thundering thoroughfare
Rich folk roll on cushions softly swelling
To the week-day feast and Sunday prayer?
Yea, who prowl there, hunger-nipped and pallid,
Breathing nightmares limned upon the gloom?
'Tis but human rubbish, gaunt and squalid,
Whom their country spurns for lack of room.
In their devious track we mutely follow,
Mutely climb dim flights of oozy stairs,
Where through gap-toothed, mizzling roof the yellow
Pestilent fog blends with the fetid air.
Through the unhinged door's discordant slamming
Ring the gruesome sounds of savage strife—[97]
Howls of babes, the drunken father's damning,
Counter-cursing of the shrill-tongued wife.
Children feebly crying on their mother
In a wailful chorus—"Give us food!"
Man and woman glaring at each other
Like two gaunt wolves with a famished brood.
Till he snatched a stick, and, madly staring,
Struck her blow on blow upon the head;
And she, reeling back, gasped, hardly caring—
"Ah, you've done it now, Jim"—and was dead.
Dead—dead—dead—the miserable creature—
Never to feel hunger's cruel fang
Wring the bowels of rebellious nature
That her infants might be spared the pang.
"Dead! Good luck to her!" The man's teeth chattered,
Stone-still stared he with blank eyes and hard,
Then, his frame with one big sob nigh shattered,
Fled—and cut his throat down in the yard.[98]
Dark the night—the children wail forsaken,
Crane their wrinkled necks and cry for food,
Drop off into fitful sleep, or waken
Trembling like a sparrow's ravished brood.
Dark the night—the rain falls on the ashes,
Feebly hissing on the feeble heat,
Filters through the ceiling, drops in splashes
On the little children's naked feet.
Dark the night—the children wail forsaken—
Is there none, ah, none, to heed their moan?
Yea, at dawn one little one is taken,
Four poor souls are left, but one is gone.
Gone—escaped—flown from the shame and sorrow
Waiting for them at life's sombre gate,
But the hand of merciless to-morrow
Drags the others shuddering to their fate.

But one came—a girlish thing—a creature
Flung by wanton hands 'mid lust and crime—[99]
A poor outcast, yet by right of nature
Sweet as odour of the upland thyme.
Scapegoat of a people's sins, and hunted,
Howled at, hooted to the wilderness,
To that wilderness of deaf hearts, blunted
To the depths of woman's dumb distress.
Jetsam, flotsam of the monster city,
Spurned, defiled, reviled, that outcast came
To those babes that whined for love and pity,
Gave them bread bought with the wage of shame.
Gave them bread, and gave them warm, maternal
Kisses not on sale for any price:
Yea, a spark, a flash of some eternal
Sympathy shone through those haunted eyes.
Ah, perchance through her dark life's confusion,
Through the haste and taste of fevered hours,
Gusts of memory on her youth's pollution
Blew forgotten scents of faded flowers.[100]
And she saw the cottage near the wild wood,
With its lichened roof and latticed panes,
Strayed once more through golden fields of childhood,
Hyacinth dells and hawthorn-scented lanes.
Heard once more the song of nesting thrushes
And the blackbird's long mellifluous note,
Felt once more the glow of maiden blushes
Burn through rosy cheek and milkwhite throat
In that orchard where the apple blossom
Lightly shaken fluttered on her hair,
As the heart was fluttering in her bosom
When her sweetheart came and kissed her there.
Often came he in the lilac-laden
Moonlit twilight, often pledged his word;
But she was a simple country-maiden,
He the offspring of a noble lord.[101]
Fading lilacs May's farewell betoken,
Fledglings fly and soon forget the nest;
Lightly may a young man's vows be broken,
And the heart break in a woman's breast.
Gathered like a sprig of summer roses
In the dewy morn and flung away,
To the girl the father's door now closes,
Let her shelter henceforth how she may.
Who will house the miserable mother
With her child, a helpless castaway!
"I, am I the keeper of my brother?"
Asks smug virtue as it turns to pray!
Lovely are the earliest Lenten lilies,
Primrose pleiads, hyacinthine sheets;
Stripped and rifled from their pastoral valleys,
See them sold now in the public streets!
Other flowers are sold there besides posies—
Eyes may have the hyacinth's glowing blue,[102]
Rounded cheeks the velvet bloom of roses,

28

Taper necks the rain-washed lily's hue.
But a rustic blossom! Love and duty
Bound up in a child whom hunger slays!
Ah! but one thing still is left her—beauty
Fresh, untarnished yet—and beauty pays.
Beauty keeps her child alive a little,
Then it dies—her woman's love with it—
Beauty's brilliant sceptre, ah, how brittle,
Drags her daily deeper down the pit.
Ruin closes o'er her—hideous, nameless;
Each fresh morning marks a deeper fall;
Till at twenty—callous, cankered, shameless,
She lies dying at the hospital.
Drink, more drink, she calls for—her harsh laughter
Grates upon the meekly praying nurse,
Eloquent about her soul's hereafter:
"Souls be blowed!" she sings out with a curse.[103]
And so dies, an unrepenting sinner—
Pitched into her pauper's grave what time
That most noble lord rides by to dinner
Who had wooed her in her innocent prime.
And in after-dinner talk he preaches
Resignation—o'er his burgundy—
Till a grateful public dubs his speeches
Oracles of true philanthropy.
Peace ye call this? Call this justice, meted
Equally to rich and poor alike?
Better than this peace the battle's heated
Cannon-balls that ask not whom they strike!
Better than this masquerade of culture
Hiding strange hyæna appetites,
The frank ravening of the raw-necked vulture
As its beak the senseless carrion smites.
What of men in bondage, toiling blunted
In the roaring factory's lurid gloom?[104]
What of cradled infants starved and stunted?
What of woman's nameless martyrdom?
The all-seeing sun shines on unheeding,
Shines by night the calm, unruffled moon,
Though the human myriads, preying, bleeding,
Put creation harshly out of tune.
"Hence, ah, hence"—I sobbed in quivering passion—
"From these fearful haunts of fiendish men!
Better far the plain, carnivorous fashion
Which is practised in the lion's den."
And I fled—yet staggering still did follow
In the footprints of my shrouded guide—
To the sea-caves echoing with the hollow
Immemorial moaning of the tide.
Sinking, swelling roared the wintry ocean,
Pitch-black chasms struck with flying blaze,
As the cloud-winged storm-sky's sheer commotion
Showed the blank Moon's mute Medusa face[105]
White o'er wastes of water—surges crashing
Over surges in the formless gloom,

29

And a mastless hulk, with great seas washing
Her scourged flanks, pitched toppling to her doom.
Through the crash of wave on wave gigantic,
Through the thunder of the hurricane,
My wild heart in breaking shrilled with frantic
Exultation—"Chaos come again!
Yea, let earth be split and cloven asunder
With man's still accumulating curse—
Life is but a momentary blunder
In the cycle of the Universe.
"Yea, let earth with forest-belted mountains,
Hills and valleys, cataracts and plains,
With her clouds and storms and fires and fountains,
Pass with all her rolling sphere contains,
Melt, dissolve again into the ocean,
Ocean fade into a nebulous haze!"[106]
And I sank back without sense or motion
'Neath the blank Moon's mute Medusa face.
Moments, years, or ages passed, when, lifting
Freezing lids, I felt the heavens on high,
And, innumerable as the sea-sands drifting,
Stars unnumbered drifted through the sky.
Rhythmical in luminous rotation,
In dædalian maze they reel and fly,
And their rushing light is Time's pulsation
In his passage through Eternity.
Constellated suns, fresh lit, declining,
Were ignited now, now quenched in space,
Rolling round each other, or inclining
Orb to orb in multi-coloured rays.
Ever showering from their flaming fountains
Light more light on each far-circling earth,
Till life stirred crepuscular seas, and mountains
Heaved convulsive with the throes of birth.[107]
And the noble brotherhood of planets,
Knitted each to each by links of light,
Circled round their suns, nor knew a minute's
Lapse or languor in their ceaseless flight.
And pale moons and rings and burning splinters
Of wrecked worlds swept round their parent spheres,
Clothed with spring or sunk in polar winters
As their sun draws nigh or disappears.
Still new vistas of new stars—far dwindling—
Through the firmament like dewdrops roll,
Torches of the Cosmos which enkindling
Flash their revelation on the soul.
Yea, One spake there—though nor form nor feature
Shown—a Voice came from the peaks of time:—
"Wilt thou judge me, wilt thou curse me, Creature
Whom I raised up from the Ocean slime?
"Long I waited—ages rolled o'er ages—
As I crystallized in granite rocks,[108]
Struggling dumb through immemorial stages,
Glacial æons, fiery earthquake shocks.
In fierce throbs of flame or slow upheaval,

Speck by tiny speck, I topped the seas,
Leaped from earth's dark womb, and in primeval
Forests shot up shafts of mammoth trees.
"Through a myriad forms I yearned and panted,
Putting forth quick shoots in endless swarms—
Giant-hoofed, sharp-tusked, or finned or planted
Writhing on the reef with pinioned arms.
I have climbed from reek of sanguine revels
In Cimmerian wood and thorny wild,
Slowly upwards to the dawnlit levels
Where I bore thee, oh my youngest Child!
"Oh, my heir and hope of my to-morrow,
I—I draw thee on through fume and fret,
Croon to thee in pain and call through sorrow,
Flowers and stars take for thy alphabet.[109]
Through the eyes of animals appealing,
Feel my fettered spirit yearn to thine,
Who, in storm of will and clash of feeling,
Shape the life that shall be—the divine.
"Oh, redeem me from my tiger rages,
Reptile greed, and foul hyæna lust;
With the hero's deeds, the thoughts of sages,
Sow and fructify this passive dust;
Drop in dew and healing love of woman
On the bloodstained hands of hungry strife,
Till there break from passion of the Human
Morning-glory of transfigured life.
"I have cast my burden on thy shoulder;
Unimagined potencies have given
That from formless Chaos thou shalt mould her
And translate gross earth to luminous heaven.
Bear, oh, bear the terrible compulsion,
Flinch not from the path thy fathers trod,[110]
From Man's martyrdom in slow convulsion
Will be born the infinite goodness—God."
Ceased the Voice: and as it ceased it drifted
Like the seashell's inarticulate moan;
From the Deep, on wings of flame uplifted,
Rose the sun rejoicing and alone.
Laughed in light upon the living ocean,
Danced and rocked itself upon the spray,
And its shivered beams in twinkling motion
Gleamed like star-motes of the Milky Way.
And beside me in the golden morning
I beheld my shrouded phantom-guide;
But no longer sorrow-veiled and mourning—
It became transfigured by my side.
And I knew—as one escaped from prison
Sees old things again with fresh surprise—
It was Love himself, Love re-arisen
With the Eternal shining through his eyes.[111]
[112]

POEMS OF THE OPEN AIR.

"Therefore all seasons shall be sweet to thee,
Whether the summer clothe the general earth
With greenness, or the redbreast sit and sing
Betwixt the tufts of snow on the bare branch."
S. T. Coleridge.
[113]

THE SOWER.
The winds had hushed at last as by command;
The quiet sky above,
With its grey clouds spread o'er the fallow land,
Sat brooding like a dove
There was no motion in the air, no sound
Within the tree-tops stirred,
Save when some last leaf, fluttering to the ground,
Dropped like a wounded bird:
Or when the swart rooks in a gathering crowd
With clamorous noises wheeled,
Hovering awhile, then swooped with wranglings loud
Down on the stubbly field.[114]
For now the big-thewed horses, toiling slow
In straining couples yoked,
Patiently dragged the ploughshare to and fro
Till their wet haunches smoked.
Till the stiff acre, broken into clods,
Bruised by the harrow's tooth,
Lay lightly shaken, with its humid sods
Ranged into furrows smooth.
There looming lone, from rise to set of sun,
Without or pause or speed,
Solemnly striding by the furrows dun,
The sower sows the seed.
The sower sows the seed, which mouldering,
Deep coffined in the earth,
Is buried now, but with the future spring
Will quicken into birth.[115]
Oh, poles of birth and death! Controlling Powers
Of human toil and need!
On this fair earth all men are surely sowers,
Surely all life is seed!
All life is seed, dropped in Time's yawning furrow,
Which with slow sprout and shoot,
In the revolving world's unfathomed morrow,
Will blossom and bear fruit.[116]

A SPRING SONG.
Dark sod pierced by flames of flowers,
Dead wood freshly quickening,
Bright skies dusked with sudden showers,
Lit by rainbows on the wing.
Cuckoo calls and young lambs' bleating
Nimble airs which coyly bring
Little gusts of tender greeting
From shy nooks where violets cling.

Half-fledged buds and birds and vernal
Fields of grass dew-glistening;
Evanescent life's eternal
Resurrection, bridal Spring![117]

APRIL RAIN.
The April rain, the April rain,
Comes slanting down in fitful showers,
Then from the furrow shoots the grain,
And banks are fledged with nestling flowers;
And in grey shaw and woodland bowers
The cuckoo through the April rain
Calls once again.
The April sun, the April sun,
Glints through the rain in fitful splendour,
And in grey shaw and woodland dun
The little leaves spring forth and tender
Their infant hands, yet weak and slender,
For warmth towards the April sun,
One after one.[118]
And between shower and shine hath birth
The rainbow's evanescent glory;
Heaven's light that breaks on mists of earth!
Frail symbol of our human story,
It flowers through showers where, looming hoary,
The rain-clouds flash with April mirth,
Like Life on earth.
[119]

THE SLEEPING BEAUTY.
There was intoxication in the air;
The wind, keen blowing from across the seas,
O'er leagues of new-ploughed land and heathery leas,
Smelt of wild gorse whose gold flamed everywhere.
An undertone of song pulsed far and near,
The soaring larks filled heaven with ecstasies,
And, like a living clock among the trees,
The shouting cuckoo struck the time of year.
For now the Sun had found the earth once more,
And woke the Sleeping Beauty with a kiss;
Who thrilled with light of love in every pore,
Opened her flower-blue eyes, and looked in his.
Then all things felt life fluttering at their core—
The world shook mystical in lambent bliss.[120]

APPLE-BLOSSOM.
Blossom of the apple trees!
Mossy trunks all gnarled and hoary,
Grey boughs tipped with rose-veined glory,
Clustered petals soft as fleece
Garlanding old apple trees!

33

How you gleam at break of day!
When the coy sun, glancing rarely,
Pouts and sparkles in the pearly
Pendulous dewdrops, twinkling gay
On each dancing leaf and spray.
Through your latticed boughs on high,
Framed in rosy wreaths, one catches
Brief kaleidoscopic snatches[121]
Of deep lapis-lazuli
In the April-coloured sky.
When the sundown's dying brand
Leaves your beauty to the tender
Magic spells of moonlight splendour,
Glimmering clouds of bloom you stand,
Turning earth to fairyland.
Cease, wild winds, O, cease to blow!
Apple-blossom, fluttering, flying,
Palely on the green turf lying,
Vanishing like winter snow;
Swift as joy to come and go.[122]

THE MUSIC-LESSON.
A thrush alit on a young-leaved spray,
And, lightly clinging,
It rocked in its singing
As the rapturous notes rose loud and gay;
And with liquid shakes,
And trills and breaks,
Rippled through blossoming boughs of May.
Like a ball of fluff, with a warm brown throat
And throbbing bosom,
'Mid the apple-blossom,
The new-fledged nestling sat learning by rote
To echo the song
So tender and strong,
As it feebly put in its frail little note.[123]
O blissfullest lesson amid the green grove!
The low wind crispeth
The leaves, where lispeth
The shy little bird with its parent above;
Two voices that mingle
And make but a single
Hymn of rejoicing in praise of their love.[124]

THE TEAMSTER.
With slow and slouching gait Sam leads the team;
He stoops i' the shoulders, worn with work not years;
One only passion has he, it would seem—
The passion for the horses which he rears:
He names them as one would some household pet,
May, Violet.
He thinks them quite as sensible as men;
As nice as women, but not near so skittish;

34

He fondles, cossets, scolds them now and then,
Nay, gravely talks as if they knew good British:
You hear him call from dawn to set of sun,
"Goo back! Com on!"[125]
Sam never seems depressed nor yet elate,
Like Nature's self he goes his punctual round;
On Sundays, smoking by his garden gate,
For hours he'll stand, with eyes upon the ground,
Like some tired cart-horse in a field alone,
And still as stone.
Yet, howsoever stolid he may seem,
Sam has his tragic background, weird and wild
Like some adventure in a drunkard's dream.
Impossible, you'd swear, for one so mild:
Yet village gossips dawdling o'er their ale
Still tell the tale.
In his young days Sam loved a servant-maid,
A girl with happy eyes like hazel brooks
That dance i' the sun, cheeks as if newly made
Of pouting roses coyly hid in nooks,
And warm brown hair that wantoned into curl:
A fresh-blown girl.[126]
Sam came a-courting while the year was blithe,
When wet browed mowers, stepping out in tune,
With level stroke and rhythmic swing of scythe,
Smote down the proud grass in the pomp of June,
And wagons, half-tipped over, seemed to sway
With loads of hay.
The elder bush beside the orchard croft
Brimmed over with its bloom like curds and cream;
From out grey nests high in the granary loft
Black clusters of small heads with callow scream
Peered open-beaked, as swallows flashed along
To feed their young.
Ripening towards the harvest swelled the wheat,
Lush cherries dangled 'gainst the latticed panes;
The roads were baking in the windless heat,
And dust had floured the glossy country lanes,
One sun-hushed, light-flushed Sunday afternoon
The last of June.[127]
When, with his thumping heart all out of joint,
And pulses beating like a stroller's drum,
Sam screwed his courage to the sticking point
And asked his blushing sweetheart if she'd come
To Titsey Fair; he meant to coax coy May
To name the day.
But her rich master snapped his thumb and swore
The girl was not for him! Should not go out!
And, whistling to his dogs, slammed-to the door
Close in Sam's face, and left him dazed without
In the fierce sunshine, blazing in his path
Like fire of wrath.
Unheeding, he went forth with hot wild eyes
Past fields of feathery oats and wine-red clover;
Unheeded, larks soared singing to the skies,

Or rang the plaintive cry of rising plover;
Unheeded, pheasants with a startled sound
Whirred from the ground.[128]
On, on he went by acres full of grain,
By trees and meadows reeling past his sight,
As to a man whirled onwards in a train
The land with spinning hedgerows seems in flight;
At last he stopped and leant a long, long while
Against a stile.
Hours passed; the clock struck ten; a hush of night,
In which even wind and water seemed at peace;
But here and there a glimmering cottage light
Shone like a glowworm through the slumberous trees;
Or from some far-off homestead through the dark
A watch-dog's bark.
But all at once Sam gave a stifled cry:
"There's fire," he muttered, "fire upon the hills!"[129]
No fire—but as the late moon rose on high
Her light looked smoke-red as through belching mills:
No fire—but moonlight turning in his path
To fire of wrath.
He looked abroad with eyes that gave the mist
A lurid tinge above the breadths of grain
Owned by May's master. Then he shook his fist,
Still muttering, "Fire!" and measured o'er again
The road he'd come, where, lapped in moonlight, lay
Huge ricks of hay.
There he paused glaring. Then he turned and waned
Like mist into the misty, moon-soaked night,
Where the pale silvery fields were blotched and stained
With strange fantastic shadows. But what light
Is that which leaps up, flickering lithe and long,
With licking tongue![130]
Hungry it darts and hisses, twists and turns,
And with each minute shoots up high and higher,
Till, wrapped in flames, the mighty hayrick burns
And sends its sparks on to a neighbouring byre,
Where, frightened at the hot, tremendous glow,
The cattle low.
And rick on rick takes fire; and next a stye,
Whence through the smoke the little pigs rush out;
The house-dog barks; then, with a startled cry,
The window is flung open, shout on shout
Wakes the hard-sleeping farm where man and maid
Start up dismayed.
And with wild faces wavering in the glare,
In nightcaps, bedgowns, clothes half huddled on
Some to the pump, some to the duck-pond tear
In frantic haste, while others splashing run
With pails, or turn the hose with flame-scorched face
Upon the blaze.[131]
At last, when some wan streaks began to show
In the chill darkness of the sky, the fire
Went out, subdued but for the sputtering glow
Of sparks among wet ashes. Barn and byre

Were safe, but swallowed all the summer math
By fire of wrath.
Still haggard from the night's wild work and pale,
Farm-men and women stood in whispering knots,
Regaled with foaming mugs of nut-brown ale;
Firing his oaths about like vicious shots,
The farmer hissed out now and then: "Gad damn!
It's that black Sam."
They had him up and taxed him with the crime;
Denying naught, he sulked and held his peace;
And so, a branded convict, in due time,
Handcuffed and cropped, they shipped him over-seas:
Seven years of shame sliced from his labourer's life
As with a knife.[132]
But through it all the image of a girl
With hazel eyes like pebbled waters clear,
And warm brown hair that wantoned into curl,
Kept his heart sweet through many a galling year,
Like to a bit of lavender long pressed
In some black chest.
At last his time was up, and Sam returned
To his dear village with its single street,
Where, in the sooty forge, the fire still burned,
As, hammering on the anvil, red with heat,
The smith wrought at a shoe with tongues aglow,
Blow upon blow.
There stood the church, with peals for death and birth,
Its ancient spire o'ertopping ancient trees,
And there the graves and mounds of unknown earth,
Gathered like little children round its knees;[133]
There was "The Bull," with sign above the door,
And sanded floor.
Unrecognized Sam took his glass of beer,
And picked up gossip which the men let fall:
How Farmer Clow had failed, and one named Steer
Had taken on the land, repairs and all;
And how the Kimber girl was to be wed
To Betsy's Ned.
Sam heard no more, flung down his pence, and took
The way down to the well-remembered stile;
There, in the gloaming by the trysting brook,
He came upon his May—with just that smile
For sheep-faced Ned, that light in happy eyes:
Oh, sugared lies!
He came upon them with black-knitted brows
And clenched brown hands, and muttered huskily:[134]
"Oh, little May, are those your true love's vows
You swore to keep while I was over-sea?"
Then crying, turned upon the other one,
"Com on, com on."
Then they fell to with faces set for fight,
And hit each other hard with rustic pride;
But Sam, whose arm with iron force could smite,
Knocked his cowed rival down, and won his bride.
May wept and smiled, swayed like a wild red rose

37

As the wind blows.
She married Sam, who loved her with a wild
Strong love he could not put to words—too deep
For her to gauge; but with her first-born child
May dropped off, flower-like, into the long sleep,
And left him nothing but the memory of
His little love.[135]
Since then the silent teamster lives alone,
The trusted headman of his master Steer;
One only passion seems he still to own—
The passion for the foals he has to rear;
And still the prettiest, full of life and play,
Is little May.
[136]

A HIGHLAND VILLAGE.
Clear shining after the rain,
The sun bursts the clouds asunder,
And the hollow-rumbling thunder
Groans like a loaded wain
As, deep in the Grampians yonder,
He grumbles now and again.
Whenever the breezes shiver
The leaves where the rain-drops quiver,
Each bough and bush and brier
Breaks into living fire,
Till every tree is bright
With blossom bursts of light.[137]
From golden roof and spout
Brown waters gurgle and splutter,
And rush down the flooded gutter
Where the village children shout,
As barefoot they splash in and out
The water with tireless patter.
The bald little Highland street
Is all alive and a-glitter;
The air blows keen and sweet
From the field where the swallows twitter;
Old wives on the doorsteps meet,
At the corner the young maids titter.
And the reapers hasten again,
Ere quite the daylight wane
To shake out the barley sheaves;
While through the twinkling leaves
The harvest moon upheaves
Clear shining after the rain.[138]

ON A FORSAKEN LARK'S NEST.
Lo, where left 'mid the sheaves, cut down by the iron-fanged reaper,
Eating its way as it clangs fast through the wavering wheat,
Lies the nest of a lark, whose little brown eggs could not keep her
As she, affrighted and scared, fled from the harvester's feet.

Ah, what a heartful of song that now will never awaken,
Closely packed in the shell, awaited love's fostering,
That should have quickened to life what, now a-cold and forsaken,
Never, enamoured of light, will meet the dawn on the wing.[139]
Ah, what pæans of joy, what raptures no mortal can measure,
Sweet as honey that's sealed in the cells of the honey-comb,
Would have ascended on high in jets of mellifluous pleasure,
Would have dropped from the clouds to nest in its gold-curtained home.
Poor, pathetic brown eggs! Oh, pulses that never will quicken!
Music mute in the shell that hath been turned to a tomb!
Many a sweet human singer, chilled and adversity-stricken,
Withers benumbed in a world his joy might have helped to illume.[140]

REAPERS.

Sun-tanned men and women, toiling there together;
Seven I count in all, in yon field of wheat,
Where the rich ripe ears in the harvest weather
Glow an orange gold through the sweltering heat.
Busy life is still, sunk in brooding leisure:
Birds have hushed their singing in the hushed tree-tops;
Not a single cloud mars the flawless azure;
Not a shadow moves o'er the moveless crops;
In the glassy shallows, that no breath is creasing,
Chestnut-coloured cows in the rushes dank[141]
Stand like cows of bronze, save when they flick the teasing
Flies with switch of tail from each quivering flank.
Nature takes a rest—even her bees are sleeping,
And the silent wood seems a church that's shut;
But these human creatures cease not from their reaping
While the corn stands high, waiting to be cut.[142]

APPLE-GATHERING.

Essex flats are pink with clover,
Kent is crowned with flaunting hops,
Whitely shine the cliffs of Dover,
Yellow wave the Midland crops;
Sussex Downs the flocks grow sleek on,
But, for me, I love to stand
Where the Herefordshire beacon
Watches o'er his orchard land.
Where now sun, now shadow dapples—
As it wavers in the breeze—
Clumps of fresh-complexioned apples
On the heavy-laden trees:[143]
Red and yellow, streaked and hoary,
Russet-coated, pale or brown—
Some are dipped in sunset glory,
And some painted by the dawn.
What profusion, what abundance!
Not a twig but has its fruits;
High in air some in the sun dance,
Some lie scattered near the roots.
These the hasty winds have taken

Are a green, untimely crop;
Those by burly rustics shaken
Fall with loud resounding plop.
In this mellow autumn weather,
Ruddy 'mid the long green grass,
Heaped-up baskets stand together,
Filled by many a blowsy lass.[144]
Red and yellow, streaked and hoary,
Pile them on the granary floors,
Till the yule-log's flame in glory
Loudly up the chimney roars;
Till gay troops of children, lightly
Tripping in with shouts of glee,
See ripe apples dangling brightly
On the red-lit Christmas-tree.[145]

THE SONGS OF SUMMER.
The songs of summer are over and past!
The swallow's forsaken the dripping eaves;
Ruined and black 'mid the sodden leaves
The nests are rudely swung in the blast:
And ever the wind like a soul in pain
Knocks and knocks at the window-pane.
The songs of summer are over and past!
Woe's me for a music sweeter than theirs—
The quick, light bound of a step on the stairs,
The greeting of lovers too sweet to last:
And ever the wind like a soul in pain
Knocks and knocks at the window-pane.[146]

AUTUMN TINTS.
Coral-coloured yew-berries
Strew the garden ways,
Hollyhocks and sunflowers
Make a dazzling blaze
In these latter days.
Marigolds by cottage doors
Flaunt their golden pride,
Crimson-punctured bramble leaves
Dapple far and wide
The green mountain-side.[147]
Far away, on hilly slopes
Where fleet rivulets run,
Miles on miles of tangled fern,
Burnished by the sun,
Glow a copper dun.
For the year that's on the wane,
Gathering all its fire,
Flares up through the kindling world
As, ere they expire,
Flames leap high and higher.[148]

GREEN LEAVES AND SERE.

Three tall poplars beside the pool
Shiver and moan in the gusty blast,
The carded clouds are blown like wool,
And the yellowing leaves fly thick and fast.
The leaves, now driven before the blast,
Now flung by fits on the curdling pool,
Are tossed heaven-high and dropped at last
As if at the whim of a jabbering fool.
O leaves, once rustling green and cool!
Two met here where one moans aghast
With wild heart heaving towards the past:
Three tall poplars beside the pool.[149]

THE HUNTER'S MOON.

The Hunter's Moon rides high,
High o'er the close-cropped plain;
Across the desert sky
The herded clouds amain
Scamper tumultuously,
Chased by the hounding wind
That yelps behind.
The clamorous hunt is done,
Warm-housed the kennelled pack;
One huntsman rides alone
With dangling bridle slack;
He wakes a hollow tone,
Far echoing to his horn
In clefts forlorn.[150]
The Hunter's Moon rides low,
Her course is nearly sped.
Where is the panting roe?
Where hath the wild deer fled?
Hunter and hunted now
Lie in oblivion deep:
Dead or asleep.[151]

THE PASSING YEAR.

No breath of wind stirs in the painted leaves,
The meadows are as stirless as the sky,
Like a Saint's halo golden vapours lie
Above the restful valley's garnered sheaves.
The journeying Sun, like one who fondly grieves,
Above the hills seems loitering with a sigh,
As loth to bid the fruitful earth good-bye,
On these hushed hours of luminous autumn eves.
There is a pathos in his softening glow,
Which like a benediction seems to hover
O'er the tranced earth, ere he must sink below
And leave her widowed of her radiant Lover,
A frost-bound sleeper in a shroud of snow
While winter winds howl a wild dirge above her.[152]

THE ROBIN REDBREAST.

The year's grown songless! No glad pipings thrill
The hedge-row elms, whose wind-worn branches shower
Their leaves on the sere grass, where some late flower
In golden chalice hoards the sunlight still.
Our summer guests, whose raptures used to fill
Each apple-blossomed garth and honeyed bower,
Have in adversity's inclement hour
Abandoned us to bleak November's chill.
But hearken! Yonder russet bird among
The crimson clusters of the homely thorn[153]
Still bubbles o'er with little rills of song—
A blending of sweet hope and resignation:
Even so, when life of love and youth is shorn,
One friend becomes its last, best consolation.[154]

THE RED SUNSETS, 1883.

The boding sky was charactered with cloud,
The scripture of the storm—but high in air,
Where the unfathomed zenith still was bare,
A pure expanse of rose-flushed violet glowed
And, kindling into crimson light, o'erflowed
The hurrying wrack with such a blood-red glare,
That heaven, igniting, wildly seemed to flare
On the dazed eyes of many an awe-struck crowd.
And in far lands folk presaged with blanched lips
Disastrous wars, earthquakes, and foundering ships
Such whelming floods as never dykes could stem,
Or some proud empire's ruin and eclipse:
Lo, such a sky, they cried, as burned o'er them
Once lit the sacking of Jerusalem![155]

THE RED SUNSETS, 1883.

The twilight heavens are flushed with gathering light,
And o'er wet roofs and huddling streets below
Hang with a strange Apocalyptic glow
On the black fringes of the wintry night.
Such bursts of glory may have rapt the sight
Of him to whom on Patmos long ago
The visionary angel came to show
That heavenly city built of chrysolite.
And lo, three factory hands begrimed with soot,
Aflame with the red splendour, marvelling stand,
And gaze with lifted faces awed and mute.
Starved of earth's beauty by Man's grudging hand,
O toilers, robbed of labour's golden fruit,
Ye, too, may feast in Nature's fairyland.[156]

ON THE LIGHTHOUSE AT ANTIBES.

A stormy light of sunset glows and glares
Between two banks of cloud, and o'er the brine

Thy fair lamp on the sky's carnation line
Alone on the lone promontory flares:
Friend of the Fisher who at nightfall fares
Where lurk false reefs masked by the hyaline
Of dimpling waves, within whose smile divine
Death lies in wait behind Circean snares.
The evening knows thee ere the evening star;
Or sees thy flame sole Regent of the bight,
When storm, hoarse rumoured by the hills afar,
Makes mariners steer landward by thy light,
Which shows through shock of hostile nature's war
How man keeps watch o'er man through deadliest night.[157]

CAGNES.
ON THE RIVIERA.
In tortuous windings up the steep incline
The sombre street toils to the village square,
Whose antique walls in stone and moulding bear
Dumb witness to the Moor. Afar off shine,
With tier on tier, cutting heaven's blue divine,
The snowy Alps; and lower the hills are fair,
With wave-green olives rippling down to where
Gold clusters hang and leaves of sunburnt vine.
You may perchance, I never shall forget
When, between twofold glory of land and sea,
We leant together o'er the old parapet,
And saw the sun go down. For, oh, to me,
The beauty of that beautiful strange place
Was its reflection beaming from your face.[158]

A WINTER LANDSCAPE.
All night, all day, in dizzy, downward flight,
Fell the wild-whirling, vague, chaotic snow,
Till every landmark of the earth below,
Trees, moorlands, roads, and each familiar sight
Were blotted out by the bewildering white.
And winds, now shrieking loud, now whimpering low,
Seemed lamentations for the world-old woe
That death must swallow life, and darkness light.
But all at once the rack was blown away,
The snowstorm hushing ended in a sigh;
Then like a flame the crescent moon on high
Leaped forth among the planets; pure as they,
Earth vied in whiteness with the Milky Way:
Herself a star beneath the starry sky.[159]
[160]

LOVE IN EXILE.

"Whatever way my days decline,
I felt and feel, tho' left alone,
His being working in mine own,
The footsteps of his life in mine."

Lord Tennyson.
[161]

SONGS.

I.

Thou walkest with me as the spirit-light
Of the hushed moon, high o'er a snowy hill,
Walks with the houseless traveller all the night,
When trees are tongueless and when mute the rill.
Moon of my soul, O phantasm of delight,
Thou walkest with me still.
The vestal flame of quenchless memory burns
In my soul's sanctuary. Yea, still for thee
My bitter heart hath yearned, as moonward yearns
Each separate wave-pulse of the clamorous sea:
My Moon of love, to whom for ever turns
The life that aches through me.[162]

II.

I was again beside my Love in dream:
Earth was so beautiful, the moon was shining;
The muffled voice of many a cataract stream
Came like a love-song, as, with arms entwining,
Our hearts were mixed in unison supreme.
The wind lay spell-bound in each pillared pine,
The tasselled larches had no sound or motion,
As my whole life was sinking into thine—
Sinking into a deep, unfathomed ocean
Of infinite love—uncircumscribed, divine.[163]
Night held her breath, it seemed, with all her stars:
Eternal eyes that watched in mute compassion
Our little lives o'erleap their mortal bars,
Fused in the fulness of immortal passion,
A passion as immortal as the stars.
There was no longer any thee or me;
No sense of self, no wish or incompleteness;
The moment, rounded to Eternity,
Annihilated time's destructive fleetness:
For all but love itself had ceased to be.[164]

III.

I am athirst, but not for wine;
The drink I long for is divine,
Poured only from your eyes in mine.
I hunger, but the bread I want,
Of which my blood and brain are scant,
Is your sweet speech, for which I pant.
I am a-cold, and lagging lame,
Life creeps along my languid frame;
Your love would fan it into flame.
Heaven's in that little word—your love!

44

It makes my heart coo like a dove,
My tears fall as I think thereof.[165]

IV.

I would I were the glow-worm, thou the flower,
That I might fill thy cup with glimmering light;
I would I were the bird, and thou the bower,
To sing thee songs throughout the summer night.
I would I were a pine tree deeply rooted,
And thou the lofty, cloud-beleaguered rock,
Still, while the blasts of heaven around us hooted,
To cleave to thee and weather every shock.
I would I were the rill, and thou the river;
So might I, leaping from some headlong steep,
With all my waters lost in thine for ever,
Be hurried onwards to the unfathomed deep.[166]
I would—what would I not? O foolish dreaming!
My words are but as leaves by autumn shed,
That, in the faded moonlight idly gleaming,
Drop on the grave where all our love lies dead.[167]

V.

Dost thou remember ever, for my sake,
When we two rowed upon the rock-bound lake?
How the wind-fretted waters blew their spray
About our brows like blossom-falls of May
One memorable day?
Dost thou remember the glad mouth that cried—
"Were it not sweet to die now side by side,
To lie together tangled in the deep
Close as the heart-beat to the heart—so keep
The everlasting sleep?"[168]
Dost thou remember? Ah, such death as this
Had set the seal upon my heart's young bliss!
But, wrenched asunder, severed and apart,
Life knew a deadlier death: the blighting smart
Which only kills the heart.[169]

VI.

O moon, large golden summer moon,
Hanging between the linden trees,
Which in the intermittent breeze
Beat with the rhythmic pulse of June!
O night-air, scented through and through
With honey-coloured flower of lime,
Sweet now as in that other time
When all my heart was sweet as you!
The sorcery of this breathing bloom
Works like enchantment in my brain,
Till, shuddering back to life again,
My dead self rises from its tomb.[170]
And, lovely with the love of yore,

Its white ghost haunts the moon-white ways;
But, when it meets me face to face,
Flies trembling to the grave once more.[171]

VII.

Why will you haunt me unawares,
And walk into my sleep,
Pacing its shadowy thoroughfares,
Where long-dried perfume scents the airs,
While ghosts of sorrow creep,
Where on Hope's ruined altar-stairs,
With ineffectual beams,
The Moon of Memory coldly glares
Upon the land of dreams?
My yearning eyes were fain to look
Upon your hidden face;
Their love, alas! you could not brook,
But in your own you mutely took
My hand, and for a space[172]
You wrung it till I throbbed and shook,
And woke with wildest moan
And wet face channelled like a brook
With your tears or my own.[173]

VIII.

When you wake from troubled slumbers
With a dream-bewildered brain,
And old leaves which no man numbers
Chattering tap against the pane;
And the midnight wind is wailing
Till your very life seems quailing
As the long gusts shudder and sigh:
Know you not that homeless cry
Is my love's, which cannot die,
Wailing through Eternity?
When beside the glowing embers,
Sitting in the twilight lone,
Drop on drop you hear November's
Melancholy monotone,[174]
As the heavy rain comes sweeping,
With a sound of weeping, weeping,
Till your blood is chilled with fears;
Know you not those falling tears,
Flowing fast through years on years,
For my sobs within your ears?
When with dolorous moan the billows
Surge around where, far and wide,
Leagues on leagues of sea-worn hollows
Throb with thunders of the tide,
And the weary waves in breaking
Fill you, thrill you, as with aching
Memories of our love of yore
Where you pace the sounding shore,

46

Hear you not, through roll and roar,
Soul call soul for evermore?[175]

IX.
In a lonesome burial-place
Crouched a mourner white of face;
Wild her eyes—unheeding
Circling pomp of night and day—
Ever crying, "Well away,
Love lies a-bleeding!"
And her sighs were like a knell,
And her tears for ever fell,
With their warm rain feeding
That purpureal flower, alas!
Trailing prostrate in the grass,
Love lies a-bleeding.[176]
Through the yews' black-tufted gloom
Crimson light dripped on the tomb,
Funeral shadows breeding:
In the sky the sun's light shed
Dyed the earth one awful red—
Love lies a-bleeding.
Came grey mists, and blanching cloud
Bore one universal shroud;
Came the bowed moon leading,
From the infinite afar
Star that rumoured unto star—
Love lies a-bleeding.[177]

X.
On life's long round by chance I found
A dell impearled with dew,
Where hyacinths, gushing from the ground,
Lent to the earth heaven's native hue
Of holy blue.
I sought that plot of azure light
Once more in gloomy hours;
But snow had fallen overnight
And wrapped in mortuary white
My fairy ring of flowers.[178]

XI.
Ah, yesterday was dark and drear,
My heart was deadly sore;
Without thy love it seemed, my Dear,
That I could live no more.
And yet I laugh and sing to-day;
Care or care not for me,
Thou canst not take the love away
With which I worship thee.
And if to-morrow, Dear, I live,
My heart I shall not break:

47

For still I hold it that to give
Is sweeter than to take.[179]

XII.
Yea, the roses are still on fire
With the bygone heat of July,
Though the least little wind drifting by
Shake a rose-leaf or two from the brier,
Be it never so soft a sigh.
Ember of love still glows and lingers
Deep at the red heart's smouldering core;
With the sudden passionate throb of yore
We shook as our eyes and clinging fingers
Met once only to meet no more.[180]

XIII.
We met as strangers on life's lonely way,
And yet it seemed we knew each other well;
There was no end to what thou hadst to say,
Or to the thousand things I found to tell.
My heart, long silent, at thy voice that day
Chimed in my breast like to a silver bell.
How much we spoke, and yet still left untold
Some secret half revealed within our eyes:
Didst thou not love me once in ages old?
Had I not called thee with importunate cries,
And, like a child left sobbing in the cold,
Listened to catch from far thy fond replies?[181]
We met as strangers, and as such we part;
Yet all my life seems leaving me with thine;
Ah, to be clasped once only heart to heart,
If only once to feel that thou wert mine!
These lips are locked, and yet I know thou art
That all in all for which my soul did pine.[182]

XIV.
You make the sunshine of my heart
And its tempestuous shower;
Sometimes the thought of you is like
A lilac bush in flower,
Yea, honey-sweet as hives in May.
And then the pang of it will strike
My bosom with a fiery smart,
As though love's deeply planted dart
Drained all its life away.
My thoughts hum round you, Dear, like bees
About a bank of thyme,
Or round the yellow blossoms of
The heavy-scented lime.[183]
Ah, sweeter you than honeydew,
Yet dark the ways of love,
For it has robbed my soul of peace,

48

And marred my life and turned heart's-ease
Into funereal rue.[184]

XV.
Dear, when I look into your eyes
My hurts are healed, my heart grows whole;
The barren places in my soul,
Like waste lands under April skies,
Break into flower beneath your eyes.
Ah, life grows lovely where you are;
Only to think of you gives light
To my dark heart, within whose night
Your image, though you bide afar,
Glows like a lake-reflected star.[185]
Dare I crave more than only this:
A thrill of love, a transient smile
To gladden all my world awhile?
No more, alas! Is mortal bliss
Not transient as a lover's kiss?[186]

XVI.
Ah, if you knew how soon and late
My eyes long for a sight of you,
Sometimes in passing by my gate
You'd linger until fall of dew,
If you but knew!
Ah, if you knew how sick and sore
My life flags for the want of you,
Straightway you'd enter at the door
And clasp my hand between your two,
If you but knew!
Ah, if you knew how lost and lone
I watch and weep and wait for you,
You'd press my heart close to your own
Till love had healed me through and through,
If you but knew![187]

XVII.
Your looks have touched my soul with bright
Ineffable emotion;
As moonbeams on a stormy night
Illume with transitory light
A seagull on her lonely flight
Across the lonely ocean.
Fluttering from out the gloom and roar,
On fitful wing she flies,
Moon-white above the moon-washed shore;
Then, drowned in darkness as before,
She's lost, as I when lit no more
By your beloved eyes.[188]

49

XVIII.

Oh, brown Eyes with long black lashes,
Young brown Eyes,
Depths of night from which there flashes
Lightning as of summer skies,
Beautiful brown Eyes!
In your veiled mysterious splendour
Passion lies
Sleeping, but with sudden tender
Dreams that fill with vague surmise
Beautiful brown Eyes.[189]
All my soul, with yearning shaken,
Asks in sighs—
Who will see your heart awaken,
Love's divine sunrise
In those young brown Eyes?[190]

XIX.

Once on a golden day,
In the golden month of May,
I gave my heart away—
Little birds were singing.
I culled my heart in truth,
Wet with the dews of youth,
For love to take, forsooth—
Little flowers were springing.
Love sweetly laughed at this,
And between kiss and kiss
Fled with my heart in his:
Winds warmly blowing.[191]
And with his sun and shower
Love kept my heart in flower,
As in the greenest bower
Rose richly glowing.
Till, worn at evensong,
Love dropped my heart among
Stones by the way ere long;
Misprizèd token.
There in the wind and rain,
Trampled and rent in twain,
Ne'er to be whole again,
My heart lies broken.[192]

XX.

What magic is there in thy mien,
What sorcery in thy smile,
Which charms away all cark and care,
Which turns the foul days into fair,
And for a little while
Changes this disenchanted scene
From the sere leaf into the green,
Transmuting with love's golden wand
This beggared life to fairyland?

50

My heart goes forth to thee, oh friend,
As some poor pilgrim to a shrine,
A pilgrim who has come from far[193]
To seek his spirit's folding star,
And sees the taper shine;
The goal to which his wanderings tend,
Where want and weariness shall end,
And kneels ecstatically blest
Because his heart hath entered rest.[194]

HEART'S-EASE.
As opiates to the sick on wakeful nights,
As light to flowers, as flowers in poor men's rooms,
As to the fisher when the tempest glooms
The cheerful twinkling of his village lights;
As emerald isles to flagging swallow flights,
As roses garlanding with tendrilled blooms
The unweeded hillocks of forgotten tombs,
As singing birds on cypress-shadowed heights,
Thou art to me—a comfort past compare—
For thy joy-kindling presence, sweet as May
Sets all my nerves to music, makes away
With sorrow and the numbing frost of care,
Until the influence of thine eyes' bright sway
Has made life's glass go up from foul to fair.[195]

UNTIMELY LOVE.
Peace, throbbing heart, nor let us shed one tear
O'er this late love's unseasonable glow;
Sweet as a violet blooming in the snow,
The posthumous offspring of the widowed year,
That smells of March when all the world is sere,
And, while around the hurtling sea-winds blow—
Which twist the oak and lay the pine tree low—
Stands childlike in the storm and has no fear.
Poor helpless blossom orphaned of the sun,
How could it thus brave winter's rude estate?
Oh love, more helpless love, why bloom so late,
Now that the flower-time of the year is done?
Since thy dear course must end when scarce begun,
Nipped by the cold touch of untoward fate.[196]

THE AFTER-GLOW.
It is a solemn evening, golden-clear—
The Alpine summits flame with rose-lit snow
And headlands purpling on wide seas below,
And clouds and woods and arid rocks appear
Dissolving in the sun's own atmosphere
And vast circumference of light, whose slow
Transfiguration—glow and after-glow—

51

Turns twilight earth to a more luminous sphere.
Oh heart, I ask, seeing that the orb of day
Has sunk below, yet left to sky and sea
His glory's spiritual after-shine:
I ask if Love, whose sun hath set for thee,
May not touch grief with his memorial ray,
And lend to loss itself a joy divine?[197]

L'ENVOI.
Thou art the goal for which my spirit longs;
As dove on dove,
Bound for one home, I send thee all my songs
With all my love.
Thou art the haven with fair harbour lights;
Safe locked in thee,
My heart would anchor after stormful nights
Alone at sea.
Thou art the rest of which my life is fain,
The perfect peace;
Absorbed in thee the world, with all its pain
And toil, would cease.[198]
Thou art the heaven to which my soul would go!
O dearest eyes,
Lost in your light you would turn hell below
To Paradise.
Thou all in all for which my heart-blood yearns!
Yea, near or far—
Where the unfathomed ether throbs and burns
With star on star,
Or where, enkindled by the fires of June,
The fresh earth glows,
Blushing beneath the mystical white moon
Through rose on rose—
Thee, thee I see, thee feel in all live things,
Beloved one;
In the first bird which tremulously sings
Ere peep of sun;[199]
In the last nestling orphaned in the hedge,
Rocked to and fro,
When dying summer shudders in the sedge,
And swallows go;
When roaring snows rush down the mountain-pass,
March floods with rills,
Or April lightens through the living grass
In daffodils;
When poppied cornfields simmer in the heat
With tare and thistle,
And, like winged clouds above the mellow wheat,
The starlings whistle;
When stained with sunset the wide moorlands glare
In the wild weather,
And clouds with flaming craters smoke and flare
Red o'er red heather;[200]
When the bent moon, on frostbound midnights waking,

Leans to the snow
Like some world-mother whose deep heart is breaking
O'er human woe.
As the round sun rolls red into the ocean,
Till all the sea
Glows fluid gold, even so life's mazy motion
Is dyed with thee:
For as the wave-like years subside and roll,
O heart's desire,
Thy soul glows interfused within my soul,
A quenchless fire.
Yea, thee I feel, all storms of life above,
Near though afar;
O thou my glorious morning star of love,
And evening star.

Printed in Great Britain
by Amazon